The Guide to Owning
American Treefrogs

Jerry G. Walls

CONTENTS

For Kenny, Lauren, Dillon, Matthew, and Harrison

Title page: The exceptionally clean and bright markings of *Hyla leucophyllata*, the Hourglass Treefrog, make it one of the most popular of the tropical treefrogs available to hobbyists. Photo: R. D. Bartlett

RE 150

© T.F.H. Publications, Inc.

Distributed in the UNITED STATES to the Pet Trade by T.F.H. Publications, Inc., 1 TFH Plaza, Neptune City, NJ 07753; on the Internet at www.tfh.com; in CANADA by Rolf C. Hagen Inc., 3225 Sartelon St., Montreal, Quebec H4R 1E8; Pet Trade by H & L Pet Supplies Inc., 27 Kingston Crescent, Kitchener, Ontario N2B 2T6; in ENGLAND by T.F.H. Publications, PO Box 74, Havant PO9 5TT; in AUSTRALIA AND THE SOUTH PACIFIC by T.F.H. (Australia), Pty. Ltd., Box 149, Brookvale 2100 N.S.W., Australia; in NEW ZEALAND by Brooklands Aquarium Ltd., 5 McGiven Drive, New Plymouth, RD1 New Zealand; in SOUTH AFRICA by Rolf C. Hagen S.A. (PTY.) LTD., P.O. Box 201199, Durban North 4016, South Africa; in JAPAN by T.F.H. Publications. Published by T.F.H. Publications, Inc.

MANUFACTURED IN THE
UNITED STATES OF AMERICA
BY T.F.H. PUBLICATIONS, INC.

TREEFROGS EVERYWHERE

Some of my earliest herp memories are of treefrogs. It's hard to grow up in Louisiana without noticing these big-eyed, sucker-fingered frogs that are drawn to lights like moths are drawn to flames. Like most other frogs, our native treefrogs are very vocal beasties, quonking and quacking and whistling their way through life and seeming to celebrate every change of the weather or mood. In the southern U.S. some treefrog or another is actively calling most of the year, avoiding (with a few exceptions) only the few weeks of freezing weather you get every year or two.

Even in the northern U.S. and southern Canada treefrogs have moved quickly to reoccupy territory they lost to the glaciers and permafrost until only a few thousand years ago, and their calls today can be heard north to Hudson Bay and even southernmost Alaska.

What are these little frogs that we so familiarly call treefrogs? If you look around a bit, you'll find that every continent has its "treefrogs," though they are not necessarily related to the frogs we know in the U.S. Basically, common folk everywhere tend to call any small frog that climbs

You could say that a treefrog is any frog that climbs trees, and you wouldn't be far wrong. *Hyla calcarata* of South America displays the typical foot structure of the American treefrogs, family Hylidae.

and has big disks at the ends of the fingers and toes "frogs of the trees" or shrubs or bushes, or whatever. In the Old World (i.e., anything that isn't the Americas, the New World) the "treefrogs" belong to many families or larger groups of frogs, especially the Rhacophoridae in southern Asia, the Hyperoliidae in Africa, and the Pelodryadidae in Australia and New Guinea. "Our" treefrogs all belong to the family Hylidae, a tremendous group that also is found from southern Europe (and barely into northern Africa) across non-tropical Asia to southern China and the cool mountains of northern Southeast Asia, plus Korea and Japan.

The family is based on the genus *Hyla*—the typical treefrogs, so-called, which is the only member of the family in Europe, Asia, and northern Africa. The fossil record indicates that the Hylidae originated in the Americas at least 35 million years ago. From this remote ancestor came a literal plethora of American treefrogs extending from permafrost zones in the north to areas of Antarctic storms and impassable deserts in the south. At some time about 25 million years ago, one or more species of *Hyla* managed to cross from North America into Asia, where it and its direct descendants spread westward toward Europe. Even today all the European and Asian hylids are very similar and closely related, and taxonomists argue as to whether they should recognize

In most of Africa and tropical Asia the treefrogs belong to the families Rhacophoridae and Hyperoliidae. *Rhacophorus pardalis*, one of the flying frogs of tropical Asia, bears a strong resemblance to some American treefrogs yet belongs to a very different family, Rhacophoridae.

Usually identified as *Hyla chinensis*, this pretty treefrog from Vietnam and southern China is closely related to the European *H. arborea*. The similarities to the western American *Hyla regilla* also are strong.

Photo: W. P. Mara

about two dozen species or just three or four species with many subspecies.

The typical treefrogs thus are a distinctly American group if we ignore the few Old World species. On the American continents and islands they have developed into three very distinctive subfamilies, the Hylinae, Phyllomedusinae, and Hemiphractinae, that except for tradition might be best considered full families. Recently tagged on to the family have been the pseudids, aquatic South American frogs noted for their unusual and sometimes gigantic tadpoles and generally kept as a full family. Because it is hard to find a reasonable coverage of the pseudids, I've chosen to include them in this book, though admittedly this is just an excuse to give you a page or two on these true oddballs that sometimes end up in the pet shops.

WHAT ABOUT AUSTRALIA?

Before I try to tell you how to recognize a hylid treefrog in the broad sense and what makes them hylids but not African hyperoliids or Asian rhacophorids, a few quick words on the New Guinea and Australian treefrogs are in order. These 160 or more species, found from eastern Indonesia over all of Australia and introduced into New Zealand and New Caledonia, include one of the most popular terrarium frogs, White's Treefrog, *Pelodryas caeruleus* (or *Litoria caerulea*). [For a brief introduction to the group, see *Reptile Hobbyist*, April, 1998.] The Australian treefrogs differ from the other Old World hylids and the American hylids by a few details of the muscles in the throat plus an incredible diversity of body form, including many species that lack obvious climbing pads and spend their life on the ground or in the water. It has been suggested by several scientists that these Australian treefrogs evolved independently from local Australian ancestors that now are placed in the family Myobatrachidae. I suspect that this is correct, as there is no evidence that the treefrogs of China, etc., ever crossed the Equator to invade Australia. For this reason I find it convenient to recognize a family Pelodryadidae distinct from the Hylidae—not that it has anything to do with this book, but just thought I'd cut off the "why didn't you mention that treefrogs live in Australia, too?" letters and save you some postage or phone bills.

A BIG SUCKER HERE, A LITTLE SUCKER THERE

Hylidae is one of the most complicated of the frog families. Even after you get rid of the Australian treefrogs, you still are left with some 600 species of frogs, all but 50 or so that look very much alike. These frogs are arranged into about 35 genera (a few doubtful and some certainly waiting to be split) and three subfamilies. These figures are a bit misleading, because half the species in the family are in one genus—*Hyla*—that resists being

Litoria gracilenta is one of several dozen southern tropical treefrogs of the Old World. Found from Indonesia to Australia, they now are placed in their own family, Pelodryadidae. Hobbyists know White's Treefrog, *Pelodryas caeruleus*, best.

Leaf-frogs, including the famous Red-eye, *Agalychnis callidryas*, are members of the hylid subfamily Phyllomedusinae. Notice that the pupil of the eye is vertical, not horizontal as in the rest of the family.

Photo: Marian Bacon

split and is found over the entire range of the family in both the Old and New Worlds.

But just what is a hylid treefrog? Well, the family is distinguished mostly by details of the skeleton at the most technical level, but to the average hobbyist treefrogs are best distinguished by having distinct climbing pads or suckers at the tips of all the fingers and toes. There are a few exceptions to this, but there aren't as many sucker-less treefrogs as you might expect. (The U.S. *Acris*, the cricket frogs, is the most familiar example.) In all the genera except those of the subfamily Phyllomedusinae, the leaf-frogs, the pupil of the eye is horizontal in position, which will distinguish American hylids from many Asian and African look-alikes. Additionally, if you look closely at the fingers or toes of a hylid, you'll notice that there is a slight angle between the pad and the digit. This angle is caused by a small piece of cartilage, the intercalary element, that gives the pad a bit more flexibility. Few other groups of frogs have this intercalary cartilage in combination with climbing pads and horizontal pupils.

How do treefrogs hang upside down and climb around freely? In moist surroundings they use the adhesion of water between the belly and a smooth surface to hang on to glass and similar surfaces, but their pads are a much more reliable way to hang in there. Under high

Yes, this treefrog has red eyes, but notice the horizontal pupils. *Duellmanohyla uranochroa* is one of a small group of Central American treefrogs, subfamily Hylinae, that often have bright red eyes.

magnification, the underside of each pad can be seen to be covered with projecting hair-like skin cells strongly anchored in the base of the pad. Around each projecting cell are depressed cells that secrete a thick fluid. The combined area of this fluid plus its thick nature allow the frog to adhere even to dry surfaces in dry air.

Hylids vary greatly in size, from dwarfs just over half an inch long to massive giants well over 5 inches in body length. With virtually no exceptions, all have long, slender arms and legs and long fingers and toes with broad webbing between the toes of the hind feet. Most have moderately short, broad snouts and large, bulging eyes with white, golden, to blackish or even red irises. In a few species there are small parotoid glands behind the head, though they are never as well marked as in the toads. However, in many species the skin of the back is rough, pebbly to slightly warty, and it is not uncommon to run across the common name "treetoad" for such species. In fact, the skin of many treefrogs is loaded with glands of various types that secrete a variety of chemicals; some species of *Phrynohyas* and *Phyllomedusa* can cause intense pain and heart arrhythmia if licked or accidentally touched to mucous tissue in the eyes, mouth, or nose. It is likely that all treefrogs produce an array of distasteful and perhaps dangerous chemicals, so it is best to never put your fingers near your face

after handling any hylid—you could get a very unpleasant surprise. Years ago I accidentally rubbed an eye while holding a common Gray Treefrog (*Hyla versicolor*) and thought I would go blind or temporarily insane from the pain. Be careful!

NOW, HERE'S MY PLAN...
It obviously is impossible to make much headway covering 600 species in just 64 pages, so this book is at best an introduction to a subject that would require several volumes. Thus I'm just going to hit the highlights, with the emphasis on the species you are likely to be able to collect personally in the United States or find in the pet shops on occasion. After a few pages on basic care of the "average" treefrog, I'll try to cover many of the 30 species of treefrogs found in the U.S., after which I'll mention a few of the most familiar treefrogs found in the tropics, both on the mainland and in the Caribbean. Since I've already written a small book (*Red-eyes and Other Leaf-frogs*, RE-139, T.F.H.) on the leaf-frogs, subfamily Phyllomedusinae, the coverage of the red-eyes and the monkey-frogs will be limited to the most commonly seen species. Lastly we'll talk a bit about the tongue-twister hemiphractines, the brooding treefrogs, and the pseudids with their unique tadpoles. This doesn't leave me many words to allocate to each group, so I guess we'd better get started...after a few words on treefrog care.

BASIC TREEFROG CARE

Because American treefrogs are found over such a large range, from sub-Arctic/Antarctic to equatorial tropics, it obviously is impossible to specify how a "typical" treefrog should be maintained in the terrarium. Additionally, their lifestyles vary from species that burrow in the floor of deserts and near-deserts through those that emerge for breeding during the U.S. winter to species that live in the relatively constant temperature and humidity regimes of the tropics.

Thus I'll here treat mostly the "basic" U.S. hylids and then mention a few variants in terrarium care.

CARING FOR TYPICAL HYLIDS

Let's take as our standard a commonly sold southeastern U.S. species, the Green Treefrog, *Hyla cinerea*. This is a fairly large (over 2 inches) and not exceptionally delicate species that is active much of the year except for the middle of winter; it often reaches the pet market. Hylids from the

Perhaps the most readily available—and cheapest—treefrog is the Green, *Hyla cinerea*. Collected from the wild in tremendous numbers, they often suffer greatly during holding and shipping and must be inspected carefully before a purchase.

Photo: I. Francais

Any pet shop should have a variety of water bowls for sale, and most will be suitable for treefrogs. An artificial leaf hung over the side of a bowl may help smaller treefrogs (and crickets) leave the water more safely.

Photo: M. Walls

U.S. require conditions of moderate humidity (certainly over 40 to 60% at night, with 80% preferable for several hours a day) and moderate temperature (daytime highs in the 80°F range, dropping 10 to 15 degrees at night). They also require a shallow water bowl for keeping the skin moist and cover for security.

These conditions are not difficult to attain in a 10-gallon all-glass terrarium. Such a terrarium can easily support two or three Green Treefrogs or similar species, while a 5-gallon terrarium can house several young specimens or smaller species. Start with a simple substrate that will retain some moisture without staying wet and fungusing. An inch or two of sandy potting soil over a layer of small gravel works well, especially if you mix in some peat. Try to avoid Perlite in the mix, which may be eaten by the frogs by accident and cause gut impactions. For extra security, one corner of the terrarium can have a tray containing an inch or two of long-grain ("live") peat or a sponge that is watered each day and kept under a cover as an emergency retreat for the frogs if you should go away or forget to mist the terrarium every day. A scattering of wide-leaved plastic plants over the bottom gives cover and also assures moist microhabitats.

Place a shallow (an inch or less is best) water bowl firmly into the bottom substrate and hang some artificial plants over the edge to let the frogs enter and leave the water easily. The plants also will allow crickets to escape the water—as you will find out, crickets have a suicidal urge to enter the water bowl and drown.

Most treefrogs spend their days stuck to the glass near the top of the terrarium with the legs pulled in to help conserve moisture. A few artificial plants running up the corners of the terrarium make them more comfortable and may make the terrarium easier to clean. Treefrogs often defecate on the glass during the day, and after a week you probably will have to scrape the sides of the terrarium to avoid fungus and bacteria growing on the feces. The more the frogs defecate in plants that can be easily removed and dipped in Clorox water, the easier it is to keep the terrarium clean.

Because you want to maintain a high humidity in the terrarium, you will have to place a sheet of plastic or even glass under the usual screen lid. Sturdy plastic (colored or clear) like that used for winterizing windows is fine, cheap, and easy to cut. You do NOT want to seal the terrarium— this will lead to stagnant air, fungus, bacteria, and short lives

Misting is important in keeping treefrogs healthy. Try to mist the sides of the terrarium and the decorations rather than the frogs themselves.

for your pets. The plastic sheet should cover about half the top of the terrarium, with enough left over on the edges to allow it to be pulled over to cover more of the top during the dry days of winter. You soon will notice that the frogs do not always gather under the plastic, often preferring to rest in the drier areas. Even in nature these and many other treefrogs can be found resting exposed to weak sunlight on broad-leaved plants near water, so they do not always want moist conditions. As a rule, if you keep the water bowl topped up and changed at least once or twice a week, a daily misting with room-temperature water will suffice to keep the frogs happily humid. Curiously, Green Treefrogs and many others do not enjoy being misted directly, so try to keep the mist on the leaves if possible.

Treefrogs do not need light for long lives, and they do not like bright lights, thus the suggested use of plastic plants in the terrarium rather than using living plants with their higher light requirements. Though some larger treefrogs will "bask" under weak sunlight in nature, in the confines of a small terrarium this rapidly could lead to dehydration. However, Green Treefrogs and many other larger hylids from temperate climates will tolerate a small fluorescent light both day and night; the heat from the light starter also will help the air circulate, reducing potentially noxious growths. As to heat, the best bet is just to control the temperature of the room around the terrarium, but if necessary you can use a small under-tank heating pad to keep the temperature up during the day. Allow the temperature to drop at night, which increases the humidity. Misting lightly in the evening just as the room lights are turned off may allow some extra condensation on the plants and terrarium walls, which may simulate natural humidity cycles. Heat lights should not be used with treefrogs kept in small glass terraria as they are hard to control and could lead to dehydration. The old recommendation of sticking an aquarium heater in a jar of water to provide both heat and moisture can be tried if you wish, but such makeshift arrangements are hard to control and not really necessary for temperate treefrogs.

TROPICAL HYLIDS

Frankly, most hylids from equatorial forests and the edges of savannas can be kept much like temperate species. Just because they are from the tropics does not mean they require distinctly higher temperatures or higher humidities. Their lives are spent much like those of most temperate hylids—the day is spent sleeping in hiding in a dark, humid microhabitat such as under a leaf or in a hole in a tree trunk. With the coming of darkness they emerge to feed or mate. Activity levels often increase during periods of heavy rain or persistent dew that help prevent dehydration. In the tropics many insects are active during rains, so feeding under such conditions is not difficult. In temperate hylids mating is more likely to occur during or just after rains, and the same is true for many tropical species.

However, you do have to make some concessions to longer periods of higher humidity and temperature in the terraria of many tropical treefrogs. The plastic may have to be pulled over more of the terrarium top at night and during the day, more cover may have to be provided, and you may have to mist twice a day. At night the humidity in the terrarium should approach 100% for a few hours, and it typically should not drop below 60% during the day. It is not necessary to maintain saturation humidity at all times, and a strong drop during the day may be beneficial. Daytime high temperatures do not have to exceed 80°F, and there should be at least a small drop (5 degrees or so) at night to help condensation from the last misting of the evening.

Tropical treefrogs often are kept and displayed in larger, high terraria that are heavily planted. This fad of planted terraria is nice, but it isn't really necessary. Frogs do not distinguish living and artificial plants, and if you are interested in animals rather than the gizmos necessary to keep a planted terrarium, so much the better in my opinion. You can build a nicer terrarium with artificials than with living plants because you don't have to worry about lighting, fertilizers, soil types, trimming plants, and other

problems that plague planted tropical terraria. Of course, planted terraria are more challenging than simple terraria, and this certainly is their appeal to some hobbyists.

ACTIVITY PROBLEMS
Well, treefrogs jump. This should be obvious, and it should be equally obvious that treefrogs can be great escape artists. Small and medium hylids can make tremendous jumps when disturbed, and they are very difficult to chase down once they escape. A small treefrog may dehydrate and die in an hour or less once loose in the dry atmosphere of your home. When you open the terrarium for feeding and servicing, be sure you know where every frog is resting before putting in your hand. Many treefrogs soon become very complacent in captivity and even can be touched or lightly brushed without moving, but don't expect this to be the norm. Be careful at all times when the lid is off the terrarium or you will lose specimens to nearly certain death.

FEEDING
The natural instinct when feeding all frogs is to give crickets of appropriate size. These insects are cultivated in tremendous numbers, are available almost everywhere at reasonable prices, and come in a size to fit almost any adult frog appetite. In nature frogs certainly do eat crickets, and treefrogs are not exceptions. It all likelihood, the domestic brown or gray cricket, *Acheta domesticus*,

Photo: I. Francais

Crickets of the correct size are the mainstay of the diet of most treefrogs. Try to feed so they are available at night. Some of the larger treefrogs, such as the Cuban, *Osteopilus septentrionalis*, may learn to take crickets offered from forceps and fingers.

will form the core of your hylid's daily diet.

However, do not make the mistake of feeding only crickets. Even if crickets are fed on a diet of calcium-supplemented greens a few hours before being placed in the terrarium, they still are too heavy in phosphorus and too low in calcium to make an exclusive long-term diet. Mealworms, the other staple food insect, are even worse because they have stronger jaws and thicker, hard to digest cuticle over the body, hiding the good stuff from the frog's digestive system.

If at all possible, at least half the diet should consist of small insects other than crickets. Waxworms make a nice weekly

Try to vary the diet of any treefrog. Flightless fruitflies are an excellent treat, especially for smaller frogs, and are inexpensive to purchase. A bit of fruit on the bottom of the terrarium will reduce escapes.

Photo: M. Walls

supplement but are too fatty for a larger part of the diet. Fruitflies and houseflies grown in cultures are excellent, and their activity will give the frogs some hunting experience and exercise. Wingless houseflies are now widely available, though not yet easy to culture at home, and are a good size for most treefrogs.

Wild-caught insects are excellent additions to the diet whenever possible. Just be careful that no dangerous insects (such as small wasps and bees or stinkbugs) or heavily plated forms (many beetles, some true bugs) are present in large numbers. Additionally, collect your insects away from yards and fields that have been subject to insecticides and also away from roadsides where pollution from oil and fuel fumes could present a problem. When feeding wild insects, remember that most small flying things head for the light and thus will fly or crawl through your ordinary mesh lids. Buy a few pieces of heavy nylon windowscreen material and place a piece under the normal lid for a few hours after feeding or you will have flies everywhere. (Old pantyhose material works well, too.) Also remember that your frogs prefer to feed at night, so present the food as the lights are about to go off in the room.

BREEDING

Very few hobbyists successfully breed any hylids, mostly because they need large areas of water in

Because of their low price, the large size of most spawns, and the difficulty of raising tadpoles, few treefrogs are successfully bred in captivity. This amplexing pair of *Hyla leucophyllata* would make a fine start to a breeding project that just could be successful and profitable.

Photo: R. D. Bartlett

No matter how rare or unusual it might be, it never is worth adding an emaciated, sickly looking treefrog to a collection. The chances of diseases spreading from the new specimen are just too great.

Photo: M. Smith

which to lay their eggs. A few forms are bred commercially using large aquaria or wading pools in greenhouses, but small-scale breeding is difficult. I'll mention breeding methods in the species discussions where reasonable.

Sexing most hylids is not difficult because males are so strongly adapted to calling to attract mates. There generally is a folded vocal sac visible under the posterior part of the throat in males. Because of the layering of skin to form the sac, even without distinctive pigment the folded sac appears darker than the surrounding skin. In many hylids males are smaller than females,

which allows them to stay on the female's back during the hours or even days in which the pair are in amplexus (mating position, the male grasping the female behind the front legs, his vent positioned above hers to easily fertilize the eggs when they are laid). Males often also have stronger colors on the sides of the throat and, especially in tropical species, may have dark pads or areas of prickles on the hands and inside the front legs to help grasp slippery females. In most hylids, only males have distinctive calls, a sure sign of sex, but often females also have weaker, less structured calls that are given during the day when disturbed or even during rains. Female calls lack the consistency of pattern of male calls, which usually are species-specific.

STARTING OUT

The beginner can find a variety of reasonably priced treefrogs at many shows, pet shops, and on dealer lists. Among the cheapest and hardiest are Cuban Treefrogs, *Osteopilus septentrionalis*, and Green Treefrogs, *Hyla cinerea*. Also readily available, though in my opinion not as hardy, are Barking Treefrogs, *Hyla gratiosa*, and Squirrel Treefrogs, *Hyla squirella*. Pacific Treefrogs, *Hyla regilla*, are hardy and tolerate lower humidities than many other treefrogs, but they are only sporadically available. The Gray Treefrogs (*Hyla versicolor* and *H. chrysoscelis*) may be available and are moderately hardy and often quite colorful.

Of the truly tropical treefrogs, the small *Hyla ebraccata* often is seen, as are a few similar relatives. Other Central American treefrogs enter the market on occasion but generally are poorly understood in the terrarium and probably are not suited for beginners. A variety of leaf-frogs, Phyllomedusinae, now appears in shops, many of these captive-bred. Though prices still are high on good material, and the specimens often are delicate until fully grown, some leaf-frogs may be

Check all new imports carefully for torn snouts. Because the less expensive treefrogs, such as these Barking Treefrogs, *Hyla gratiosa*, often are shipped in poor condition, they are a very likely source of red-leg and other contagious diseases.

Photo: I. Francais

suitable for near-beginners with some experience. I'm not quite sure how it has happened, but captive-bred specimens of hylids usually represent only the more expensive and exotic leaf-frogs; few breeders produce temperate treefrogs, low prices on wild-caught material preventing a captive-bred market from developing.

As always, be sure you set up your terrarium before making your purchase and be sure you can provide the correct foods continually. Never try to "rescue" a weak, emaciated, or obviously diseased treefrog, as you will not succeed and have a good chance of introducing diseases into your animal room. Pick only plump (for the species) specimens with no skin abrasions, bloody areas on the snout, back, or limbs, and NEVER with bloody red pustules under the thighs (possibly the contagious bacterial disease red-leg). Beware of broken legs in wild-caught specimens. Crowded dealer display tanks are a good source of infectious diseases, as are dirty terraria. Choose both your dealer and your frogs wisely.

Many treefrogs seem to do well in pairs or small groups, and it does no harm to purchase several healthy specimens at one time if you can make a good buy—and can be sure they are healthy and feeding. One frog carrying red-leg or another contagious condition, however, could lead to the death of an entire terrarium in just a few days under the crowded conditions in even a large, well-maintained terrarium. Make your selection carefully and AVOID

ANY SPECIMENS THAT MIGHT EVEN POSSIBLY BE TROUBLE. If possible, try to buy captive-bred specimens, and always quarantine new purchases for at least two weeks before adding them to the collection.

Finally, many treefrogs from the U.S. are available only if you collect your own specimens. Though most of our species are widely distributed and common, never get greedy. If you collect from mating choruses, when these frogs are easiest to find, select at most a male and two females. Spent females (those already having laid their eggs) are less likely to become eggbound in the terrarium. Commercial collecting of large numbers of males (noisy and especially easy to find) from choruses has led to rarity of some treefrogs in certain areas, and this could lead to even more legal restrictions on collecting. One species, *Hyla andersoni*, the Pine Barrens Treefrog, is so spottily distributed and uncommon it should never be collected; it also is protected over its range. Many states restrict or limit collecting of all frogs to an open season and require that you have a fishing license to keep anything.

If you keep a close eye on the treefrogs that come into the larger pet shops, you sometimes will be surprised at the variety of species available at low prices. Always select only the best specimens, never those that might be diseased or injured—regardless of rarity, and you could soon establish a great collection of these fascinating frogs.

TREEFROGS IN THE U.S. & CANADA

Though the treefrogs are a mostly tropical and subtropical family (in Mexico there are over 80 species currently recognized, while numbers increase as you head toward the Equator), the U.S. and southern Canada have a decent variety. Most lists today recognize 27 species in the family as originating in the U.S., with another three species tropical forms that just cross our southern borders. The three tropical species (one each in the genera *Osteopilus, Pternohyla,* and *Smilisca*) will be covered in the next chapter, so in this chapter we will discuss only the native species of *Acris, Hyla,* and *Pseudacris.* Even these, however, form a complicated group with many species that are familiar even to beginning hobbyists but others that rarely are collected.

Since this is not a taxonomic book and there is limited space, I suggest that you consult a standard field guide for identification details. Additionally, there is considerable controversy at the moment over just which genera to recognize for the U.S. hylids and where to place several of the species. Though I personally disagree with some of the following names, these are the U.S. treefrogs treated in this chapter, according to several recent workers:

Cricket Frog, Northern———
Acris crepitans
Cricket Frog, Southern———
Acris gryllus
Treefrog, Pine Barrens———
Hyla andersoni
Treefrog, Canyon———
Hyla arenicolor
Treefrog, Bird-voiced———
Hyla avivoca
Treefrog, California———
Hyla cadaverina
Treefrog, Cope's Gray———
Hyla chrysoscelis
Treefrog, Green———
Hyla cinerea
Treefrog, Mountain———
Hyla eximia
Treefrog, Pine Woods———
Hyla femoralis
Treefrog, Barking———
Hyla gratiosa
Treefrog, Pacific———
Hyla regilla
Treefrog, Squirrel———
Hyla squirella
Treefrog, Eastern Gray———
Hyla versicolor
Grass Frog, Little———
Pseudacris ocularis
Spring Peeper———
Pseudacris crucifer
Chorus Frog, Mountain———
Pseudacris brachyphona
Chorus Frog, Brimley's———
Pseudacris brimleyi
Chorus Frog, Spotted———
Pseudacris clarki
Chorus Frog, Upland———
Pseudacris feriarum
Chorus Frog, Illinois———
Pseudacris illinoensis
Chorus Frog, New Jersey———

Pseudacris kalmi
    Chorus Frog, Boreal————————
Pseudacris maculata
    Chorus Frog, Southern————————
Pseudacris nigrita
    Chorus Frog, Ornate————————
Pseudacris ornata
    Chorus Frog, Strecker's————————
Pseudacris streckeri
    Chorus Frog, Western————————
Pseudacris triseriata

As a rule, the U.S. treefrogs and their relatives lay large numbers of eggs (250 to 2000) in large or small jelly masses that float at the surface or are attached to vegetation. The eggs hatch in two to five days, producing tadpoles that may be as much as 2 inches in length and have high dorsal fins and rather pointed tails. Telling the tadpoles apart may require considerable skill and an identified reference collection. Most mature in 60 to 75 days, producing small, weak froglets that should be raised separately on springtails and fruitflies. None of our treefrogs are commercially captive-bred.

CRICKET FROGS

With the cricket frogs, *Acris*, we have non-tree-climbing treefrogs! These little, warty, but colorful frogs have lost the wide toe pads of other northern treefrogs and have developed to live their lives in a niche that lacks other small frogs. They are abundant at the edges of ditches, lakes, rivers, and ponds throughout the southern U.S. barely into northeastern Mexico, and are the typical inhabitants of shallow, usually weedy banks wherever you go in the South. Typical adults are an inch long (a truly gigantic female would still be under 1.5 inches), with pointed snouts, large eyes,

Though they lack obvious toe pads, cricket frogs, *Acris*, are indeed true treefrogs. These tiny frogs may be extremely abundant near almost any shallow permanent water.

Photo: Suzanne L. Collins

and relatively short hind legs. The feet are widely webbed, the toes ending in pads that are not much wider than the rest of the digits. The skin of the back is warty, and there are small warts on each side of the vent at the bases of the thighs. Few features of the color pattern are constant, but as a general rule the dark brown triangle between the eyes is accompanied by a broad dark brown oblique stripe on each side and one or two broad dark brown bands running along the back of each thigh against a whitish background. The back is brown, red, yellow, or green, often with more than one color on an individual and an irregular red, green, or yellow middorsal stripe. Any color or combination of colors may occur in a local colony.

Male cricket frogs are smaller than females, less plump, and have dark throats. Mating can take place through much of the warm months of the year, females laying several hundred small eggs (often in packets of just a few eggs at a time) in a shallow backwater that has lots of grasses or aquatic plants. The tadpoles are distinctive in usually having finely pointed tails that end in a broad black triangle. Though there is considerable turnover from predation, in captivity cricket frogs have lived about five years.

Don't get the impression that these are aquatic frogs—they are land frogs that just happen to like to live at the edge of shallow water. As you walk along the edge of a lake or ditch, cricket frogs often explode from underfoot

Across much of the eastern U.S. the common cricket frog is the Northern, *Acris crepitans*. Coloration varies greatly, as does the roughness of the back. If you can provide cricket frogs with fruitflies and other tiny insects, you may have luck keeping them.

Found only in the deep southeastern U.S., including the Florida Peninsula, the Southern Cricket Frog, *Acris gryllus*, is virtually identical in appearance and habits to the Northern Cricket Frog. Both cricket frogs are excellent jumpers and hard to keep in a small terrarium.

Photo: K. H. Switak

much like popcorn, always staying a foot or two ahead. Their jumps are unpredictable, and they often end up in the water, where they may swim to a spot of safety on an emerged leaf or dig into the mud of the bottom; within minutes they are back at the edge again, looking for the springtails, ants, flies, spiders, aphids, tiny beetles, and caterpillars that make up most of their diet. They do not feed in the water and are not specialized for aquatic prey, though they will take tiny snails and amphipods.

Northern Cricket Frogs, *Acris crepitans*, are found from New Jersey and New York to Wisconsin, then south to western Texas, northeastern Mexico, and the Gulf of Mexico. The species is absent from the Coastal Plain east of the Appalachian Mountains and from peninsular Florida. There it is replaced by the virtually identical Southern Cricket Frog, *Acris gryllus*, which ranges from southeastern Virginia to the Mississippi River, including all of Florida. Distinguishing the two species is complex.

Cricket frogs can be kept somewhat drier than other treefrogs and don't mind the sun (of course, they prefer the shade), often being active even at midday during the summer. They can be kept in roomy terraria (remember—they jump wildly and often and if excited can easily escape any tank; they also climb well by adhesion of the wet belly) with a standard substrate plus a large, shallow water bowl flush with the substrate. A few plastic plant leaves in the water will help them feel at home. Don't keep the bottom too moist or they will come down with infections. The major problem is feeding—fruitflies have worked well for some keepers, and pinhead crickets also will be taken though often not really savored. Ants are dangerous to feed, springtails are hard to culture, and spider egg cases may be hard to find. Provide a hiding spot on the bottom of the terrarium.

Cricket frogs seldom are sold as pets, though they sometimes enter the market as cheap feeder frogs. They often are sold or collected as fish bait as well. Their small size and tendency to escape make them difficult pets for most keepers, especially when small insect foods are difficult to find. However, in much of the southern U.S. they are perhaps the most conspicuous and easy to collect frogs during the warm months of the year, and there is a tendency to pick up a few to try them in the terrarium for a few weeks or months.

This calling male *Hyla cinerea* displays the clear white stripe on the side, bordered by black, typical of most members of the species. Green Treefrogs vary considerably in color and pattern individually, geographically, and with temperature and activity.

Photo: P. Freed

Barking Treefrogs, *Hyla gratiosa*, are somewhat stouter and coarser-skinned than their close relative the Green Treefrog. Notice that the stripe on the side of the body is ragged-edged and tinged with purple. Spotting on the back may come and go with temperature and mood.

GREEN TREEFROGS

Three southeastern U.S. treefrogs are mostly or all green in life, another is very similar to one of the green species, and all are easily confused. Curiously, all four appear in the hobby, and three are not uncommonly sold in pet shops. In fact, the Green Treefrog, *Hyla cinerea*, which is found from Delaware to central Texas, is one of the most commonly sold treefrogs in the shops, being collected in large numbers at breeding choruses from the Carolinas to Louisiana and shipped (sometimes in poor condition) everywhere. This is a rather large, glossy green species with a broad, sharp-edged white stripe along the side. Large females may be 2 to 2.5 inches long, with long, strong legs bearing a distinct white stripe on the outer surfaces. At night the green may turn distinctly yellowish, and in poor condition it may be a tan to grayish frog. The Barking Treefrog, *Hyla gratiosa*, is found from Delaware to the Mississippi River across the southern U.S. and is stouter in build than Green Treefrogs, to which it is closely related. (The two even hybridize on occasion.) Adults commonly are 2 inches long (but may reach almost 3 inches) and have many pale-edged dark green to blackish spots on the back and a ragged stripe on the side tinged with purple. The spots often disappear, in which case the two can be told by the rougher, finely warty skin of the Barking Treefrog. Both species sing and breed during the warmer months of the year, preferring ponds and permanent ditches in which to lay their many hundreds of eggs. Green Treefrogs lay their eggs in a large mass at the surface, while Barking Treefrogs lay mostly single eggs.

Green and Barking Treefrogs are common in pet shops and on dealer lists, often selling for only a few dollars. Unfortunately, if you cannot collect your own specimens you have to be very careful when selecting a specimen. Many are males (dark throats) collected at choruses and in a highly unstable hormonal condition that makes it difficult for them to adapt to the terrarium. Check all specimens for abrasions that could lead to bacterial infections, red-leg (pustular red areas on the thighs and posterior belly), and broken legs. Quarantine is essential. Healthy specimens, on the other hand, are hardy animals that feed well and often are quite brazen, reacting well to captivity. Few specimens are captive-bred.

The other two frogs in this group might be better called greenish treefrogs. Both the Squirrel (*H. squirella*) and the Pine Woods (*H. femoralis*) Treefrogs are small, rather slender animals abut 1.5 inches long and with long, slender legs. Squirrel Treefrogs usually are dull green with an indistinct pale stripe down the side and bright orange on the thighs and groin. Pine Woods Treefrogs, on the other hand, typically are reddish brown above with indistinct darker blotches, but they can on

Though sometimes sold as baby Green Treefrogs, the Squirrel Treefrog, *Hyla squirella*, is a distinct species that often is more brown than green. It never has a clean-edged white stripe on the side and typically has the entire hidden area of the folded legs orange.

A calling male Pine Woods Treefrog, *Hyla femoralis*. The resemblance to brown Squirrel Treefrogs is strong, but this less common species has distinct specks of orange to green color hidden in the folded legs. Given its restricted distribution in the Deep South and its elusive habits, it may be surprising to find that this species does appear in pet shops occasionally.

Photo: R. D. Bartlett

occasion be greenish. They have dark thighs and groins with many distinct round orange to greenish spots. Both are southern frogs, the Squirrel being found from eastern Texas to southeastern Virginia, while the Pine Woods extends from Virginia to the Mississippi River in Louisiana. Squirrels are almost domestic frogs, often being found in ditches and gardens and coming to the lights on houses to feed on insects, while the Pine Woods is a much more elusive frog virtually restricted to ponds and swamps in pine and cypress areas with sandy soils. Pine Woods Treefrogs are noted for forming gigantic mating choruses that can sound like an army of riveters at work. Both species appear in the hobby on occasion, the Squirrels often misidentified as young Greens.

A fifth treefrog actually belongs here: the gorgeous but strongly protected Pine Barrens Treefrog, *H. andersoni*. This bright green frog is 1.5 to 2 inches long and stout in appearance, like the Barking Treefrog. It has a broad pale to bright lavender stripe along the side from the snout through the eye and tympanum toward the groin, bordered below by a narrow yellowish line. The throat often is yellowish with small violet spots, while the groin is bright orange. This would make a pretty pet and is fairly

Photo: M. Panzella

Hyla andersoni, the Pine Barrens Treefrog, has gained considerable notoriety due to its greatly restricted distribution in just a few states. Protected by state and federal laws, it even appears on license plates.

adaptable, but its range is restricted to white cedar swamps and similar habitats in central New Jersey, the North and South Carolina borderlands, and the Florida Panhandle. It is protected in this range and not legally keepable. Even to get to see this frog, which may be locally common, is a thrill.

GRAY TREEFROGS

For many years "the" Gray Treefrog was known as *Hyla versicolor*, a species common and widely distributed from central Texas to eastern North Dakota and adjacent Canada, eastward over much of the United States (though absent from peninsular Florida). Then a dwarfed version of the Gray with a very different voice was discovered in the Deep South and it was found that "the" Gray Treefrog occurred in two different chromosome counts and call types. Today three gray treefrogs are recognized, but the group can be identified by the overall mottled back, usually gray to greenish gray with a large dark brown blotch near or in front of center. More obviously, there is a large white spot below the eye, and the groin and thighs are yellowish green (Bird-voiced Treefrog, *H. avivoca*) or orange (other two species). Bird-voiced Treefrogs have less warty skin on the back than the other two species and have a high-pitched, shrill whistle. They are found during the spring and summer breeding in flooded backwaters of swamps and oxbow lakes from Oklahoma and Illinois to South

Carolina and south. Males may call from 6 to 8 feet up in the cypress and gum trees. Tadpoles have red saddles on top of the tail.

The common gray treefrogs cannot be distinguished by any external character or by range and usually are just called the *Hyla versicolor* Complex. The Eastern Gray Treefrog is *H. versicolor*, a tetraploid species (two pairs of each set of chromosomes in each cell), while Cope's Gray Treefrog, *H. chrysoscelis*, is a diploid species with normal chromosome pairs. There are small differences between the species in the speed of male calls, but these are difficult to distinguish. These often are very warty treefrogs ("treetoads") that can exist in dry areas and often are found hiding in holes in fence posts at the edges of pastures and woodlots. Their warty skin is quite waxy and can resist drying. One or both of these species can be found almost anywhere east of the Great Plains, and they breed in almost any large expanses of open water from spring through autumn. They spend most of the day in the trees, coming to the ground at night to mate and to feed on a variety of insects and spiders. Females may lay 2000 eggs at a time, these hatching to produce tadpoles that have bright red blotches and tones in the tail fin.

Gray treefrogs sometimes appear in the pet shops (and even Bird-voiced Treefrogs pop up occasionally) and are easy to keep if healthy. They can take quite large prey insects and tolerate dry conditions better than most treefrogs—but still don't ever let

Notice the wide white spot below the eye of this tan Gray Treefrog, *Hyla versicolor* Complex. In the eastern U.S., this mark allows the species (or pair of species) to be distinguished from all other treefrogs but the Bird-voiced Treefrog. The hidden thigh surfaces tend toward orange in color.

Photo: M. Smith

their habitat dry up. Many writers have attributed distinct personalities to pet gray treefrogs, and they are noted for their acrobatic activities. Pets may get quite tame and are easily overfed. They have lived about eight years in captivity.

WESTERN TREEFROGS

The four species of treefrogs found from western Texas to the Pacific Ocean are a varied group and not often available in the shops. Their taxonomy also is confused, with some occasionally referred to *Pseudacris* and perhaps actually belonging to a distinct genus.

One species, the Mountain Treefrog, *Hyla eximia*, actually is a Mexican form that enters the U.S. in a patchy distribution in Arizona and New Mexico. This small (1 to 1.5 inches, rarely to 2 inches) species is closely related to the Pacific Treefrog, *Hyla regilla*, and is best distinguished by its more eastern range. *Hyla regilla* is an abundant and variable frog often 2 inches long and with a short dark brown stripe from the tip of the snout through the eye and tympanum to the shoulder. The belly is white but becomes yellow to the back and on the thighs, while the back color varies from brown to red or green, often with a dark triangle between the eyes. Other spotting on the back varies considerably. Pacific Treefrogs are found, sometimes abundantly, from British Columbia to the tip of Baja California, Mexico, the largest range of any western treefrog. Numerous subspecies of

Distinguished from Gray Treefrogs largely by voice, Bird-voiced Treefrogs, *Hyla avivoca*, also tend to be smaller, smoother, and often greener (especially on the backs of the thighs) than their larger cousins. The species sometimes enters the terrarium hobby.

Photo: A. Norman

The rough skin has made Gray Treefrogs the typical "tree toad" of local stories, and that name commonly appeared even in scientific papers a century ago. Among our hardiest amphibians, Gray Treefrogs, regardless of species, can make excellent pets with pleasant personalities.

Photo: M. Smith

doubtful validity are recognized. *H. regilla* can be kept much like a Green Treefrog, liking a small pan of shallow water in their tank. These two species sometimes are placed in *Pseudacris*, the chorus frogs, and may belong in their own genus along with some Mexican species.

The other two western treefrogs are warty, stout-bodied animals that lack a distinct dark mask and tend to be tan (Canyon Treefrog, *H. arenicolor*) or grayish (California Treefrog, *H. cadaverina*). The two species are very similar and were confused for many years. They are best distinguished by range— Canyon Treefrogs are found from southwestern Texas to northwestern Arizona north to Utah and south into Mexico, while California Treefrogs are restricted to southern California and the Baja Peninsula. Both species are found near desert streams and oases, so they have spotty distributions. While California Treefrogs quack like ducks, Canyon Treefrogs sound like rivet guns whirring away in the distance. Both species breed through most of the first half of the year, at least when there is sufficient water in their streams and ponds. Canyon Treefrogs sometimes are collected for the market and are quite resistant to drying out, much as in the gray treefrogs.

SPRING PEEPERS

Traditionally the Spring Peeper was considered to be a true treefrog (*Hyla*), but today it is

Pacific Treefrogs, *Hyla regilla*, are notoriously variable in color, skin texture, size, and build. Though many subspecies have been described, at the moment they are not recognized. Brown and green individuals are perhaps most common, but red specimens are not rare.

Photos: S. McKeown (top); G. & C. Merker (bottom)

assigned to the chorus frogs as *Pseudacris crucifer*; it probably will end up in its own genus, which has been called *Parapseudacris*. This is a small (seldom reaching 1.5 inches) frog of relatively stout build and of a generally pale brown color above with a characteristic dark X in the middle of the back. The toe pads are narrower than in most *Hyla*, only a bit wider than the digits. These frogs tend to breed in the early spring soon after the ice melts. In the northeastern U.S. the Spring Peeper is considered a harbinger of spring, its "peep," actually a single-note whistle, in breeding choruses being one of the first spring sounds heard. In the South it may breed from Thanksgiving through the winter. Females lay up to a thousand single eggs rather than large masses as in most other treefrogs. The range is extensive, including virtually all the U.S. east of the Great Plains, except peninsular Florida, and most of eastern Canada south of the permafrost zone.

Spring Peepers, because they often are so common over such a great range, sometimes enter the hobby market, but they are not especially easy frogs to keep. Though they feed on a wide array of small insects and spiders, they are inactive during most of the

Found near desert streams and oases from Texas to Arizona, Canyon Treefrogs, *Hyla arenicolor*, may be surprisingly common in dry habitats and do not dehydrate easily. Large, heavy-set treefrogs, they make excellent pets but are not very colorful.

Photo: R. D. Bartlett

year when the temperature reaches much over 80°F and are easily stressed under typical keeping conditions. Few specimens have lived over two years in the terrarium.

LITTLE GRASS FROGS

Though at the moment placed in the genus *Pseudacris* with the chorus frogs, the Little Grass Frog, *P. ocularis*, long has driven herpetologists crazy. Their tiny size, only half an inch to three-quarters of an inch in body length when fully mature, has been accompanied by changes in the skeleton that give it many distinctive characters. At one time it was placed in its own genus, *Limnaoedus*, and it is highly possible it will return there in the future. Regardless, this is a distinctive but easily overlooked frog of grassy pineland meadows and cypress ponds from the Virginia border barely into Alabama, including all of Florida. It looks a bit like a tiny cricket frog, including a relatively pointed snout and often a dark brown triangle between the eyes, but the hind legs are exceptionally long and slender, the back is not especially warty, and there are no dark stripes on the backs of the thighs. Coloration is simple, generally some shade of tan (reddish to yellowish) above, with a wide black stripe from the snout through the eye running to or beyond the shoulder and marked below by a pale area. The belly is white and unspotted. The toe pads are tiny but well formed and usually distinctly wider than the

Found only in southern California and the Baja Peninsula of Mexico, the California Treefrog, *Hyla cadaverina*, was not recognized as distinct from the Canyon Treefrog until some 40 or 50 years ago. It sometimes appears as *Hyla californiae* in the scientific literature.

Photo: S. McKeown

X marks the spot, at least on most Spring Peepers, *Pseudacris crucifer*. One of the most familiar frogs calling in early spring, Peepers make relatively poor pets because they are stressed by most household temperatures. Their taxonomy is badly confused.

Photo: J. E. Gerholdt

width of the digits.

These mites breed throughout the year in Florida and even in the Carolinas may be found laying in all but the coldest weeks of the year. Their call is very soft and high-pitched, hard to hear, and sounds like a tiny cricket. Males call from a few inches to several feet above the water of grassy ponds and backwaters. Females lay their eggs singly at the bottom of the pond; the tadpoles often are distinctly greenish in tone.

These are the smallest frogs in the U.S. and among the smallest in the world, which makes their keeping difficult. What do you feed a frog that any cricket could best in a fair fight? Fruitflies and springtails are your best bet, as usual, but many hobbyists find these hard to maintain. Though occasionally appearing on Florida dealer's lists as locally collected oddities, they are not generally available and are not easy to collect even where common.

COMMON CHORUS FROGS

The majority of the chorus frogs, genus *Pseudacris*, are very similar and difficult to distinguish unless you are an expert. They are slender, long-legged, generally smooth-skinned treefrogs with small toe pads not much wider than the digits. This does not stop them from being good climbers, however, and they usually call

Photo: R. D. Bartlett

Though it may be abundant locally from coastal Virginia to Alabama, the Little Grass Frog, *Pseudacris ocularis*, seldom is noticed unless breeding. At considerably less than an inch in maximum length, this is the smallest frog native to the U.S.

from tall grasses and low shrubs near temporary ponds. Typically they are pale brownish above with a wide darker brown stripe from the tip of the snout to the groin on the side and two (*P. brachyphona*) or three dark brown to blackish stripes or rows of spots down the back. A species found from Texas to Kansas, *P. clarki*, has the spots and stripes all blackish green, a distinctive color.

These frogs, though sometimes abundant locally when breeding, are secretive dwellers of the forest floor most of the year, hiding in the litter and under wood and stones. They usually emerge with the cool rains of late autumn to early spring, when the females lay large numbers of eggs in temporary ponds and ditches. At these times they can be collected in large numbers, but their small size (seldom over 1.5 inches) and usually dull colors prevent them from being shipped to the shops. They are difficult to feed, as with other small treefrogs, though taking a variety of small insects, spiders, and possibly worms. If you collect your local species at their choruses or by accident later in the year, you can try to keep them much like cricket frogs.

MASKED CHORUS FROGS

Three species of chorus frogs are quite distinct from the other species yet very similar to each other. All are exceptionally stout chorus frogs with large front legs that may be almost toad-like in breeding males. In all three species the snout is short, the eyes very large, and the skin nearly smooth to very finely warty, and there is a broad black mask running from the tip of the snout through the eye to the shoulder. The back is variously spotted with brown on a tan or grayish to bright red or green background, while the belly is white. The groin tends to be yellowish or pale orange. Unlike other American treefrogs, when cornered the masked chorus frogs burrow rapidly into loose sandy soils by using their strong front feet. They rarely are seen above ground except during the winter to spring breeding season, and they have been found to spend much of the year underground,

actively feeding there without emerging. Though stout, they are not large frogs, being 1 to 1.5 inches long, with a giant female just under 2 inches reported.

Masked chorus frogs are not commonly collected, though they have a rather large total range. The three species have non-overlapping distributions but are not easy to distinguish except for "typically marked" adults. In the southeastern U.S. (North Carolina over northern Florida just into Louisiana, always in the sandy pinelands and cypress areas) is found the reddish to greenish *Pseudacris ornata*, the Ornate Chorus Frog. It has large black spots on the sides outlined with narrow pale rings. The front legs, though strong, are not exceptionally stout. Strecker's

Over much of the eastern and central U.S. the common chorus frog is one of several species virtually identical in appearance to *Pseudacris triseriata*, the Western Chorus Frog. These long-legged little treefrogs have small pads at the ends of the digits and tend to breed during winter in much of their range.

Photo: R. T. Zappalorti

Chorus Frog, *P. streckeri*, is found in sandy prairie habitats from eastern Texas (barely into Louisiana) north into Oklahoma, northwestern Arkansas, and barely into Kansas. The front legs are extremely stout, especially in males, and there usually is a black spot below the eye, while the black spots on the sides are poorly developed. Most adults are reddish above, but many are greenish. The very similar but paler Illinois Chorus Frog, *P. illinoensis*, is restricted to scattered remnants of prairie in western Illinois and southeastern Missouri and adjacent Arkansas. Because its already sparse habitat has been almost eliminated, it is protected to some extent. Illinois and Strecker's Chorus Frogs sometimes adapt to cultivated farm lands, but in such situations they may be exposed to dangerous amounts of agricultural chemicals.

In the terrarium these tend to be secretive frogs that do little climbing and may take all their meals under cover. Given a loose substrate, they may not emerge unless "rained" on. Larger adults may take crickets as well as small earthworms and tubifex worms. Other insect foods will be accepted. They are not available in the market and seldom are personally collected.

Pseudacris nigrita, the Southern Chorus Frog, is the southeastern version of the Western Chorus Frog. It tends toward spots rather than stripes and gray and black coloration rather than tan and dark brown. Chorus frogs are notoriously tough to identify, with many individual variations and much geographic variation as well.

Photo: M. Smith

East of the Mississippi River, the masked chorus frog is *Pseudacris ornata*, the Ornate Chorus Frog. This stout and brightly patterned species varies greatly in color, but some individuals may be distinctly reddish.

Pseudacris illinoensis, the Illinois Chorus Frog, is very similar to Strecker's Chorus Frog of the southern Great Plains. Restricted to relict areas of sandy prairie along the Mississippi River, it currently is disappearing from many formerly inhabited areas.

Photo: R. D. Bartlett

TREEFROGS IN THE TROPICS

Literally hundreds of treefrogs are found south of the U.S. border, but few ever are available to hobbyists. In fact, the majority are virtually unknown even to biologists, and new species are described every year. Many are similar to common U.S. forms in general appearance, and only a few really stand out. Care of most is fairly simple, requiring a tall terrarium with a substrate that retains some humidity, a cover that keeps the tank from drying out, and preferably some tropical plantings, live or artificial. The terrarium should be misted twice a day for most commonly available forms, and a fogger may help keep the animals healthy. Most treefrogs should be kept at fairly low temperatures, 80°F or so, as they inhabit cool, well-ventilated microhabitats; many come from higher elevations.

Breeding tropical treefrogs is difficult in captivity, and the few that are bred (on an irregular basis) do best in a greenhouse situation. Remember that in the tropics breeding cycles are timed to respond to wet and dry seasons, with breeding generally beginning or reaching its peak during the rainy season (or seasons, in some areas). Though some tropical treefrogs are relatively solitary, males calling from hidden spots to attract individual females, most breed in large male-dominated choruses where males arrive a day or more before females, choose suitable mating spots around the edge of a pond, stream, or temporary body of water, and call in females with loud and species-distinct songs. Many tropical treefrogs find their mates at the water and then move by pairs into neighboring trees and shrubs while in amplexus. The eggs may be laid on plant leaves a few inches to feet above the water surface or in water as normal. Tadpoles, as in most hylids, form schools and feed on detritus. Many have distinctive color patterns, but relatively few tropical hylids have been studied well enough to easily identify random tadpoles.

Obviously the diversity of tropical treefrogs prevents me from doing more than barely scratching the surface here. I'll thus only mention the three tropical species that cross into the U.S. from the south and then a few genera and species that sometimes show up in the shops or on dealer lists. For a good introduction to tropical treefrogs, glance through *Guide to the Frogs of the Iquitos Region, Amazonian Peru*, by Rodriguez and Duellman, 1994 (Univ. Kansas Nat. Hist.

Mus.), an extremely well-illustrated guide.

FROM SOUTH OF THE BORDER

Two Mexican treefrogs, representing two genera, are represented in the U.S. fauna as rarities. One, the Lowland Burrowing Treefrog, *Pternohyla fodiens*, is found from southwestern Mexico barely into southeastern Arizona. This is a strange, terrestrial treefrog strongly modified for digging shallow burrows in sandy soils and grassy plains. The skin of the head is fused to the bones, and there is a ridge of skin across the back of the head. The back is tan with large black-edged dark brown spots. *Pternohyla*, which seldom can be found except when gathering to breed at temporary ponds after the first heavy rains of the summer, are poorly known treefrogs, but they have appeared on dealer lists occasionally, perhaps illegally.

Also just crossing the border into the U.S., this time the lower Rio Grande around Brownsville, Texas, is *Smilisca baudini*, given the rather inappropriate name Mexican Treefrog. It actually occurs widely on the Atlantic Coast from Costa Rica north and is one of the most common and adaptable tropical treefrogs. It is a large species, 2 to 2.5 inches long and heavy-bodied, with very large feet and large suckers. Like Gray Treefrogs, it has a white spot under the eye, but there also is a wide black blotch over the eardrum that usually is visible. The tan to greenish back typically has a large dark brown blotch in the front center. Most of the year

Pternohyla fodiens, a desert burrower, is relatively common in Mexico, but it barely manages to cross the U.S. border into southeastern Arizona, where it seldom is collected. Rather surprisingly, the stout-bodied Lowland Burrowing Treefrog has appeared in the hobby on occasion.

Photo: K. H. Switak

Photo: K. H. Switak

Mexican Treefrogs, *Smilisca baudini*, are abundant over much of eastern Mexico, often coming to houses and being easily collected at lights. In the U.S. the species occurs only in the lower Rio Grande region of Texas. This is one of the more toxic treefrogs, so care in handling is strongly suggested.

is spent under cover of logs, litter, rocks, and similar debris, coming out at night to feed on insects. Its habitat usually is open, dry country with only a scattering of trees and shrubs, but it is partial to banana plants where available. Breeding occurs throughout the year whenever rains bring enough water to flood dry basins and ditches. Mexican Treefrogs are reputed to make good, hardy pets, though their skin toxins may be strong enough to make handling a bit risky.

CUBAN TREEFROGS

Found widely over the island of Cuba plus the Bahamas is a large (often 3 inches or a bit more in females) brownish to grayish treefrog with extremely large climbing pads on the fingers and toes. This species, the Cuban Treefrog, *Osteopilus septentrionalis*, also occurs in the Florida Keys, perhaps naturally, and has extended its range over the southern half of Florida in the past 50 years. It now is the dominant treefrog in much of southern Florida and is easily collected, so it often appears cheaply in pet shops. The skin of the head is fused to the bones underneath, and there is a ridge of bone over the eardrum and along the upper part of the snout. Coloration usually is simple, without a distinctive pattern, but this frog has an engaging personality and is very hardy in the terrarium, so it is well worth giving it a few gallons of space. It has a voracious appetite, preferring larger insects of all

Photo: J. E. Gerholdt

Now abundant in southern Florida, the Cuban Treefrog, *Osteopilus septentrionalis*, is a rough-skinned, personable, very hardy frog that makes an excellent pet and is available cheaply. Beware of cannibalism, however.

Though most older specimens are some shade of brown with little pattern, young Cuban Treefrogs may be distinctly greenish, quite colorful animals.

Photo: M. Smith

types, and generally hunts at night, often near lights. Large specimens eat smaller frogs of their own and other species, so be careful if you try to house two specimens of unequal size together. Virtually all specimens in the shops are wild-caught, but they usually are in good condition. Breeding in captivity occurs when the frogs are given a large area (such as a child's wading pool in a greenhouse) and there is a constant drizzle. Choruses may be very loud and distracting, and females may produce thousands of eggs.

VENOMOUS TREEFROGS

The genus *Phrynohyas* sometimes shows up in the hobby in the form of the Common Venomous Treefrog, *P. venulosa*. The common and scientific names both refer to the dangerous toxins secreted by the many glands in the thick back skin. The thick, sticky white mucus is produced on handling or even just annoyance. Though the mucus of most treefrogs is irritating if it comes into contact with your eyes or lips, in this genus the mucus is dangerously toxic. If it enters your eyes, it will cause temporary blindness, and if it touches the lips, nose, or a cut, it will cause extreme pain, muscle contractions, and numbness. These frogs are best left to advanced hobbyists, or at least they should always be treated with caution.

Phrynohyas venulosa is a very stocky treefrog sometimes more than 4 inches in length (females

larger than males) and with very large hands and feet, the digits ending in exceptionally wide pads. There are broad webs on the hind feet and smaller but distinct webs between the fingers. Like the other species of the genus (which has perhaps between five and ten species), it is highly arboreal, living in the shelter of tall, leafy trees and seldom coming to the ground except to form mating choruses. It is found from southern Mexico to northern Argentina, usually in rainforest conditions, but it can tolerate drier habitats. Typically it is yellowish to pale greenish tan with a large reddish brown hourglass or U on the back and heavy barring on the hind legs. The lower lip is glossy white. The thick skin of the back is smooth to pebbly. Females lay their eggs in large sheets on the surface of ponds. Other species in the genus may lay their eggs in treeholes, avoiding the ground even for breeding.

CASQUE-HEADED TREEFROGS

For an unknown reason, many treefrog groups fuse the skin of the head to the bones of the skull underneath. Such treefrogs occur throughout the tropics on both the continent and the islands of the Caribbean, and generally it takes a second look to notice the condition. There are exceptions, however, and hobbyists vie for the occasional specimens of the more bizarre "casque-headed" treefrogs that find their way to the market. Two genera have traditionally drawn the most attention, though neither is likely to be found in

Though the pattern may be attractive and the large size appealing, beginners probably should not try to keep the Venomous Treefrog, *Phrynohyas venulosa*. When disturbed, it produces copious secretions that are dangerously toxic. Some specimens are uniformly brownish, while others may have very bumpy skin.

Photo: Marian Bacon

your ordinary pet shop.

Trachycephalus, rough-headed casque-heads, are found over much of northern and central South America, often hiding by day in bromeliads and other plants in rain forests. The three or four species may be 3 to 4 inches long and generally are brownish or reddish brown in color. The distinctive feature is the depressed, very bony head roughened with ridges of bone and often with a distinct notch at the tip of the snout. Older literature often calls these frogs by the name *Tetraprion*, a synonym.

More often available—but never common—is the Shovel-nosed Treefrog, *Triprion spatulatus*. One of two species in this Mexican genus, it is found in relatively dry, open forests and plains along the Pacific Coast of Mexico. (The second species is found on the Atlantic Coast south to Honduras.) This is one of the most bizarre frogs. Adults are 2.5 to 4 inches long, females much larger than males, with long legs and wide climbing pads. The coloration is simple, usually some shade of greenish to bronzy brown, sometimes with a broken mesh of black lines over the back, but the head is truly sensational. The bony head has a heavy ridge of bone across its back. The top of the head is saddle-shaped, with a broad, deep groove between the eyes on top of the snout. The snout itself is not elongated, but instead the edges of the upper jaws are widened into serrated, flat flanges that produce a unique

Casque-headed treefrogs have the skin of the head fused to the underlying bones. In *Trachycephalus jordani* from northwestern South America the front of the snout is not especially flared and may be notched.

Triprion petasatus from the Atlantic Coast of Mexico (the Yucatan Peninsula) and Honduras recently has entered the hobby in small numbers and has been bred in captivity. Unlike the Pacific Coast *T. spatulatus*, the back often carries large round brown spots, but the flaring of the snout is not as pronounced.

Photo: G. & C. Merker

shape. In this species there is no ridge from the eye to the nostril. This cryptic treefrog hides in holes in trees during the day, coming down only to breed. It feeds on insects and similar invertebrates of all types. Though it can tolerate quite dry keeping conditions, it is best kept in a planted terrarium with many hiding places. The genus formerly was known as *Diaglena*, which still pops up in some books.

OTHER TREEFROGS

There is room here to mention only a few tropical *Hyla* that sometimes pop up in the terrarium, chosen from the many dozen that could in theory be available. Of these, the golden-fronted treefrog group is most often seen. Comprising at least five or six similar species, three show up with some regularity. The group is found from southern Mexico to southeastern Brazil and is recognized by the presence of a broad yellow triangle on the snout (usually), protruding eyes, and generally a yellow belly. The legs are long and slender, the webbing often bright red or yellow.

The Selva Treefrog, *Hyla ebraccata*, is under 2 inches long and is imported from its Central American range on occasion. The back and legs are brown, with many white to yellow blotches forming two wide bands. Smaller brown spots are found within the yellow bands, and there is a white

Photo: A. Norman

Selva Treefrogs, *Hyla ebraccata*, still enter the hobby in decent numbers from Central America. Notice the pale spot under the eye of this pretty frog.

to yellow spot under the eye. It often is confused with the Hourglass Treefrog, *Hyla leucophyllata*, which comes from rain forests of eastern South America. Also imported on a regular basis, this delicate treefrog differs from the Selva at first glance mostly by having a very regular pattern of a pair of wide yellow bands on the sides of the brown back and two wide yellow bands on the hind leg. There are no smaller brown spots in the yellow bands. The similar *H. sarayacuensis* has dark and pale mottling on the back and very uneven edges to the yellow bands. All these frogs are relatively delicate except when kept in a heavily planted

In *Hyla sarayacuensis* the pattern is much as in the Hourglass Treefrog except all the yellow bands are rough-edged and there are small yellow spots erratically placed in the brown areas as well. Several other similar but smaller treefrogs also occur in northwestern South America.

Photo: P. Freed

As hard as it might be to believe, these two frogs both represent *Hyla leucophyllata*, the Hourglass Treefrog of South America. The common form is rich brown and yellow, but the reticulated or giraffe morph is densely spotted with brown against a whitish network. The two forms long were considered full species, the giraffe being called *H. favosa*, but they now are known to belong to a single species and may occur in the same breeding colonies.

Photos: R. D. Bartlett

The translucent yellowish green color of *Hyla punctata* contrasts with small red spots on the back and a red stripe on the side during the day, becoming overall pale reddish brown on the back at night. The eyes may have startling silver-white irises and are positioned high on the head. Though small and delicate, the Red-spotted Treefrog is imported occasionally.

Photos: R. D. Bartlett

Though many tropical treefrogs are brownish to grayish above, these otherwise dull animals may have stunning belly and leg colors. *Hyla marmorata* from the Amazon has spotted underparts, bright orange and black under the legs, and a row of white tubercles along the back edge of the legs.

Photo: R. D. Bartlett

terrarium and fed on small food.

The ghostly Red-spotted Treefrog, *Hyla punctata*, is a common species some 1.5 inches long and of delicate, almost translucent build. Found from Colombia south to Argentina near ponds in open territory (from open woods to pastures), it is unusual in having two distinctive patterns. During the day it is pale green above, pale yellow to white below, with many deep red to reddish brown spots and flecks scattered over the back; the upper side is marked with a narrow red stripe and a wider yellow stripe. At night the back becomes uniformly reddish tan (or nearly so) and the legs and sides become greenish. Imports don't need high humidity but generally are delicate.

Many Amazonian treefrogs are tiny animals and hard to find. *Hyla miyatai* is adult at well under an inch in length and was not described until 1990. The red and yellow pattern is quite distinctive.

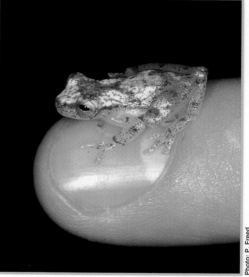

Photo: P. Freed

LEAF-FROGS: RED-EYES & COMPANY

Perhaps the most easily recognized treefrogs are the 50 or so species known as the leaf-frogs, subfamily Phyllomedusinae. Not only do most species have the fingers and toes shifted a bit so an opposable thumb or big toe is produced (often leading to a slow, hand over hand walking gait), but the pupil of the eye is vertical, compared to horizontal in other American treefrogs. The eyes themselves may be brilliant silver to deep blood-red and always are large and protruding. Technically, other differences from typical treefrogs include the presence of 26 chromosomes and a strange pigment, rhodomelanin, found in the skin; rhodomelanin also is found in some Australian treefrogs, *Litoria*. The group has unusual breeding habits, the females laying dense clusters of eggs on leaves or in the funnels of broad-leaved plants, above the water. The eggs produce tadpoles that drop into the water below the egg cluster and develop normally.

Leaf-frogs include several very popular species that are available to hobbyists on a regular basis, plus some that are imported or bred sporadically. The most popular is the Red-eyed Leaf-frog, *Agalychnis callidryas*, which is the only species likely to be affordable by the average hobbyist. The group deserves a book of its own, and in fact there actually is one. For more details about all the species of the subfamily, plus some of the basic techniques used to keep and breed them, see my book *Red-eyes and Other Leaf-frogs*, 1996 (RE-139, T.F.H.). Because that book is readily available, I'll only give you a glance at the phyllomedusines here.

RED-EYES

The most recognizable treefrog certainly is the Red-eyed Leaf-frog, *Agalychnis callidryas*, whose image decorates mugs, tee-shirts, wallpaper, utensils, and toys everywhere you look. This bright green frog with orange hands and feet has very large bright red eyes that absolutely seem to shine—when they are open. Unfortunately, this frog when seen in shops often is in poor condition and being kept poorly, so it is usually tightly hunkered up in a corner with its eyes shut and the legs pulled against the body. At 2 inches for males and 3 inches for females, it is a fairly large treefrog and conspicuous. The range includes rain forests from southern Mexico to the Colombian border, and it often is abundant locally.

If you remember that this is an

Agalychnis callidryas, the Red-eyed Leaf-frog, has become one of the most popularized amphibians during the last decade, its visage appearing on all types of products. Though bred in captivity, it still is a difficult species that seldom is suitable for beginners.

Photo: Marian Bacon

arboreal frog that is active only at night and mostly during the rainy season, it will make keeping easier. Unless breeding, it seldom ventures to the ground, so it needs a high terrarium that is relatively moist and well-ventilated and provides it with lots of cover in the form of real or artificial plants. Keep the lights low (cover the cage if necessary) and mist twice daily; a fogger unit will help. Feed in the evening on a variety of insects, not just the usual crickets, and provide vitamin and calcium supplements.

This frog and most other phyllomedusines breed during the rainy season. Males congregate in large numbers at the edges of temporary ponds and call to attract mates. They enter amplexus, and the larger female may carry the small male around for several days until actual egg-laying occurs. The female deposits a thick clump of jelly containing 50 to 100 eggs under a broad leaf overhanging the pond and the male fertilizes them. In about ten days (at 80°F) the jelly begins to dissolve and releases the young tadpoles, which slide down the leaf into the water. The tadpoles leave the water as rather dull grayish brown froglets two or three months later and take 18 months to mature. Small numbers of Red-eyes are bred in captivity, but most you will see (even the froglets) are imports that may be greatly stressed, parasitized, and weak. If you want to successfully keep this species,

Anna's Leaf-frog, *Agalychnis annae*, is an orange-eyed Central American species that occasionally is imported for the terrarium though considered delicate. All the leaf-frogs are relatively difficult to breed, which may limit their general availability.

Photo: P. Freed

The gold-spangled black eyes of Mexican Leaf-frogs, *Pachymedusa dacnicolor*, may be one of the species's most endearing traits. Recently this large leaf-frog has been captive-bred in small numbers and prices have dropped, but it still is far from common and is not generally available.

Photo: G. & C. Merker

try to get captive-bred specimens.

Other species of *Agalychnis* are seen on occasion, and recently small numbers of the green and orange *A. spurrelli*, the Gliding Leaf-frog (Costa Rica to Colombia), and the dull green and pinkish *A. lithodryas*, the Pink-sided Leaf-frog (Panama and Colombia), have been bred in captivity, but they are not widely available.

Also sporadically available is the large (females to 4 inches) Mexican Leaf-frog, *Pachymedusa dacnicolor*, a stout bright green frog with heavy legs and pale fingers and toes. The black eye is flecked with bright silver. A species of dry scrub forests of western Mexico, it tolerates relatively low humidity. Like the Red-eye, it breeds during the short, sporadic rainy season, laying masses of bluish eggs on leaves above ponds. Captive-bred specimens sometimes are available; Mexico does not allow legal exports, so wild-caught specimens probably are illegal.

PHYLLOMEDUSA

Even after several odd species are removed to other genera, there are almost 30 species of walking frogs or monkey frogs currently recognized. They form a group of variable species, ranging from tiny greenish or tan frogs with toothpick legs to 5-inch monsters with bold green and white patterns. In typical species the first and second digits are shifted and can be opposed to grasp twigs, and they tend to walk or

Photo: Marian Bacon

This glossy green Giant Monkey Frog, *Phyllomedusa bicolor*, still is young, but it has most of the distinctive adult pattern of many white circles and spots in a blackish band along the side. Formerly represented mostly by highly stressed imports, Giant Monkey Frogs now are being captive-bred for the hobby.

climb slowly, not hop away wildly like other frogs. Most are green and have bright colors hidden in the groin and behind the thighs, some with dark circles or bars. Few of the *Phyllomedusa* are widely available, though several are imported on occasion, often at high prices. They are mostly frogs of forest edges from Panama to Argentina, though some are at home in grassy pastures and high, cool mountains. Most species lay their eggs in the axils of broad-leaved plants and may twist the leaves over to produce a sealed nest. There may be water-filled infertile eggs mixed among the normal eggs, these providing necessary moisture when the environment becomes too dry; opened nests usually fail.

The Giant Monkey Frog, *Phyllomedusa bicolor*, is found over most of northern and central South America. At 5 inches (males smaller than females), this is the giant of the group. It is a thick-skinned bright green frog with a few scattered whitish pimples on the back and bright silver eyes; there is a band of black and white spots and circles along each side and black-edged white spots below the eyes. The skin of this frog produces a soup of chemicals that not only cause numbness, temporary blindness, and pain, but also appear to be psychoactive, producing hallucinations and altered moods. The secretions are used in rites of passage and hunting rituals by several South American tribes

After captive breeding succeeded, Waxy Monkey Frogs, *Phyllomedusa sauvagi*, in a matter of two years went from rare imports to fairly affordable and easy to find. Whether this large and distinctive treefrog will remain in the hobby still is uncertain, however, as few frog breeders continue working on one species for very long.

Photo: Marian Bacon

Photo: R. D. Bartlett

The evenly spaced vertical black and orange bars on the sides and thighs give *Phyllomedusa tomopterna* the common name Tiger-striped Leaf-frog. Though usually only 2 inches long and delicate, it has begun to appear on dealer lists with some frequency.

and are considered to hold some promise as a source of pharmaceuticals.

Waxy Monkey Frogs, *Phyllomedusa sauvagi*, come from dry habitats from Bolivia to Argentina. There they survive by wiping waxy compounds over the skin to reduce loss of water through the skin. Adults are about 3 inches long and have bronzy eyes. The back is rough, bluish green, and there is a white stripe along the side; the dull green belly has at least two broad white bands that may be broken into spots. This distinctive frog once was a rarity, seldom imported and sold at high prices, but recently a few breeders have successfully produced large numbers of young and the price has dropped significantly. Like most other tropical frogs, it breeds after periods of artificial rain in a moisture chamber.

Smaller *Phyllomedusa* are imported and occasionally bred in captivity. One of the most colorful is the Tiger-striped Leaf-frog, *P. tomopterna*, a rainforest species found over most of northern and central South America. This beautiful little (2 to 2.5 inches) frog is bright green above with brilliant orange on the sides and all the legs. There are short, even black bars in all the orange areas. The Orange-legged Leaf-frog, *P. hypochondrialis*, is somewhat similar, but the orange of the sides and legs is plain or has black circles or meshwork in it; there is a broad white stripe over the upper lip. Both these frogs lay their eggs in nests made from rolled leaves of plants at the edges of breeding ponds.

It is likely that other leaf-frogs will become available in the future, and some will be bred in captivity. Whether any will prove hardy enough to be kept by the average hobbyist is uncertain, and none of these frogs have a firm potential in the hobby.

LOOSE ENDS

As I promised, this chapter will just sneak a quick peek at a few of the odder treefrogs, specifically *Hemiphractus* and *Gastrotheca*, plus a few words on the pseudids, which may or may not be treefrogs. None of these frogs are common in the terrarium hobby, though a few people breed *Gastrotheca* on a small scale, occasional pseudids are imported, and many hobbyists would give at least a finger or two for a *Hemiphractus*.

BROODING TREEFROGS

Though only some 70 or so species are in the subfamily Hemiphractinae, this is one of the most intriguing of all the treefrog groups. The five genera currently recognized include some very rare and poorly understood treefrogs, some known only from very small areas in remote mountain ranges of South America. Species of *Cryptobatrachus*, *Flectonotus*, and *Stefania* are virtually unknown in the terrarium hobby, while few specimens of any of the five species of *Hemiphractus* are imported at any price. Most often seen are doubtfully identified species of *Gastrotheca*, the marsupial treefrogs.

All these strange genera share a behavioral trait as well as details of the skeleton: they all maneuver the eggs onto the back of the female during mating, the eggs becoming attached to the mother's skin and sometimes being enfolded within a blood-vessel-filled growth of skin that completely covers them. In the most primitive genera the eggs are exposed to the elements, but in *Gastrotheca* they are completely protected. The eggs develop on the mother's back, eventually hatching out as either well-developed tadpoles or gill-less froglets.

MARSUPIAL TREEFROGS

Though not especially colorful, the genus *Gastrotheca* is popular with advanced hobbyists, though little stock is maintained or bred in captivity. The genus, which contains about 50 species that are difficult to identify, is found from Panama to northern Argentina, with most of the species found in and along the Andes of western South America. They are fairly large treefrogs (often 2 inches or a bit more and fairly heavily built) that generally are greenish to brownish above with dark brown stripes on the lower sides and a pair of wide, curved brown stripes on the back. Details of color and pattern often vary greatly within a species, and even within an individual depending on temperature and activity. The eyes are large, protruding, and often bright gold, with the usual horizontal pupils of this subfamily. Males usually are distinctly smaller than females and may differ in color and pattern. In most species the hind feet are strongly developed, with very long toes that end in small to large pads. The elongated toes are used by the female to open the brood sack on the back and kick the tadpoles or young out into their new lives.

Marsupial treefrogs are noted for the presence of an enclosed egg or brood pouch on the back of the female. The pouch, which is not very visible unless filled with eggs, opens posteriorly through a small opening above the vent. (Curiously, males sometimes have folds of skin representing the female pouch.) Mating occurs on the land or in low shrubs above the water, but not in it. During mating the male produces a fluid that makes it easier for the fertilized eggs to flow into the female's pouch. Obviously a female must take a contorted position for this to happen.

The eggs incubate in the stable environment of the pouch, commonly taking 10 to 16 weeks to develop. In about half the species of the genus the eggs develop only to the tadpole stage (in as little as six weeks) before being released into a pond or the water-filled leaf axil of a bromeliad or other tropical plant. The rest of the genus hold the eggs longer

Identifying marsupial treefrogs is difficult or impossible, but it seems likely that this attractive specimen represents *Gastrotheca riobambae* from moderately high elevations in Colombia and Ecuador. This species adapts well to many terrarium conditions but must have fresh, never stagnant, air.

and release froglets. The tadpoles may take two months to perhaps a year to reach metamorphosis, the longer times in species that inhabit cool mountain habitats. In captivity they will take crumbled fish flake foods and other detritus-like foods.

Marsupial treefrogs, when available, are best kept in a heavily planted tropical terrarium at moderate temperatures (about 80°F) and moderate humidity. Mist the terrarium each day. Some species have thick, warty skin and need less water than those with thinner skin. The most common hobby species (probably *Gastrotheca riobambae* from along the Andes of Colombia and Ecuador) is quite adaptable

Close-up of eggs and young larvae being extruded from the dorsal pouch of a female *Gastrotheca marsupialis*. In nature the mother uses her exceptionally long toes to clean out the pouch.

Photo: P. Freed

because its highland habitat varies considerably. Feed on the greatest variety of small insects, spiders, pillbugs, earthworms, and similar foods available. If the terrarium is not adequately ventilated, these frogs are delicate and do not prosper.

HORNED TREEFROGS

The bizarre horned treefrogs, genus *Hemiphractus*, are found from Panama to Bolivia and generally are nearly terrestrial, though often found in shrubs along tropical trails at night. All are found in rainforest habitats at fairly high elevations and cool conditions. They are active at night and are voracious predators on other frogs, moths, and large grasshoppers. When touched, they rear back and display the large mouth, which may be bright yellow and white within. They have "teeth" near the center of the lower jaw that can inflict a painful, bloody bite if you are careless.

If you consider just the color, these are not impressive frogs—they are various shades of brown, sometimes with bands on the legs, and have many flaps of tissue that serve to camouflage the body shape. However, the shape is so bizarre it is appealing. The head is extremely long and broad, with small or large fleshy horns over the eyes and often a long horn sticking out the front of the snout as well. There are bony knobs down the center of the back that are extensions of the vertebral column, and there usually are wide toe pads on the short legs. Adults typically are 2 inches or a bit more in length.

Few *Hemiphractus* reach the hobby, but those that do sell for high prices. They are difficult to keep for very long, needing cool but humid conditions and good ventilation. A female may carry over a dozen eggs in an open pouch on the back. The large eggs are placed on the back of the female (with the aid of the male, assumedly) and held in place by mucous secretions that form a cup at the base of each egg. A female may carry from 2 to 14 eggs in an open pouch. The developing embryos have two pairs of large gills, but development takes place entirely within the egg, froglets emerging. Little is known about the details

The numerous fringes, flaps, and other projections of skin found from the tip of the snout to the backs of the legs in *Hemiphractus proboscideus* have excellent camouflage value.

Photo: R. D. Bartlett

A face only a mother—or a treefrog specialist—could love: *Hemiphractus proboscideus*, the Long-nosed Horned Treefrog. Fangs on the roof of the brightly contrasting mouth can inflict a painful bite. These are very cannibalistic frogs, something to remember if you should ever be fortunate enough to own one.

Photo: R. D. Bartlett

of breeding. Keep all specimens separately as they may be very cannibalistic—frogs of all types form the principal diet in the wild.

PARADOXICAL FROGS

Finally, just a few words about *Pseudis paradoxa*, an aquatic frog also known as the "shrinking frog." *Pseudis* is one of two genera (the other is the dwarf *Lysapsus* from Argentina and adjacent areas) assigned to the family Pseudidae, which is defined by having long rods of cartilage between the last two segments of the toes of the hind feet. The eyes are distinctly dorsal in position (looking upward, as in other aquatic frogs), and there are teeth on the upper jaws. The recent tendency is to consider the pseudids as a subfamily of

Though it bears little resemblance to a typical treefrog, some scientists now feel that the aquatic *Pseudis paradoxa* and the family Pseudidae actually represent just small modifications of basic hylid structures; they would place the paradoxical frogs in a subfamily of Hylidae.

Photo: W. P. Mara

Hylidae rather than a full family, though the adults look more like ranas than treefrogs. The pupil is horizontal. In *Pseudis*, adults commonly are almost 3 inches long in body length, and they shrink in size from gigantic tadpoles that may be more than 8 inches long.

Paradoxical Frogs are resident in many types of permanent waters from Venezuela and the Guianas over northern and central South America to Argentina. They prefer lakes, ponds, and oxbows with many aquatic plants, where they hang at the surface with the eyes and nostrils projecting above the surface. Generally they are a nice green above with a pair of blackish stripes or rows of spots down the back and a blackish stripe on the side back from the eye. The legs may be strongly spotted with black ovals, and males may have black webbing on the feet. The webbing, by the way, typically extends to the tips of the toes. Add to this silvery eyes and you have a very nice frog for the tropical aquarium—not terrarium. They like warm, shallow water with lots of plants. As a rule, they are delicate additions to the collection and seldom live for very long, perhaps because of stress during collecting and shipping.

With the Paradoxical Frog we end our discussion of the American treefrogs. Obviously I have not been able to answer all your questions or even help you identify those odd specimens from "somewhere in South America," but maybe I've given you a little bit more of an understanding of this tremendous frog family, one of the most typically American of all the frogs.

Numbers in **bold** type indicate photographs